Max on a Hill

words by Nigel Croser
illustrated by Neil Curtis

Min and Mop and Max live on a hill.

Min jumps.
Mop jumps.

But Max rolls.

"Sheep don't roll," said Min.

Min eats grass.
Mop eats grass.

But Max rolls.

"Sheep don't roll," said Mop.

A big red fox came.

Min and Mop stood still.

The fox eats sheep.

Then the fox saw lots of legs.

It looked like a monster.

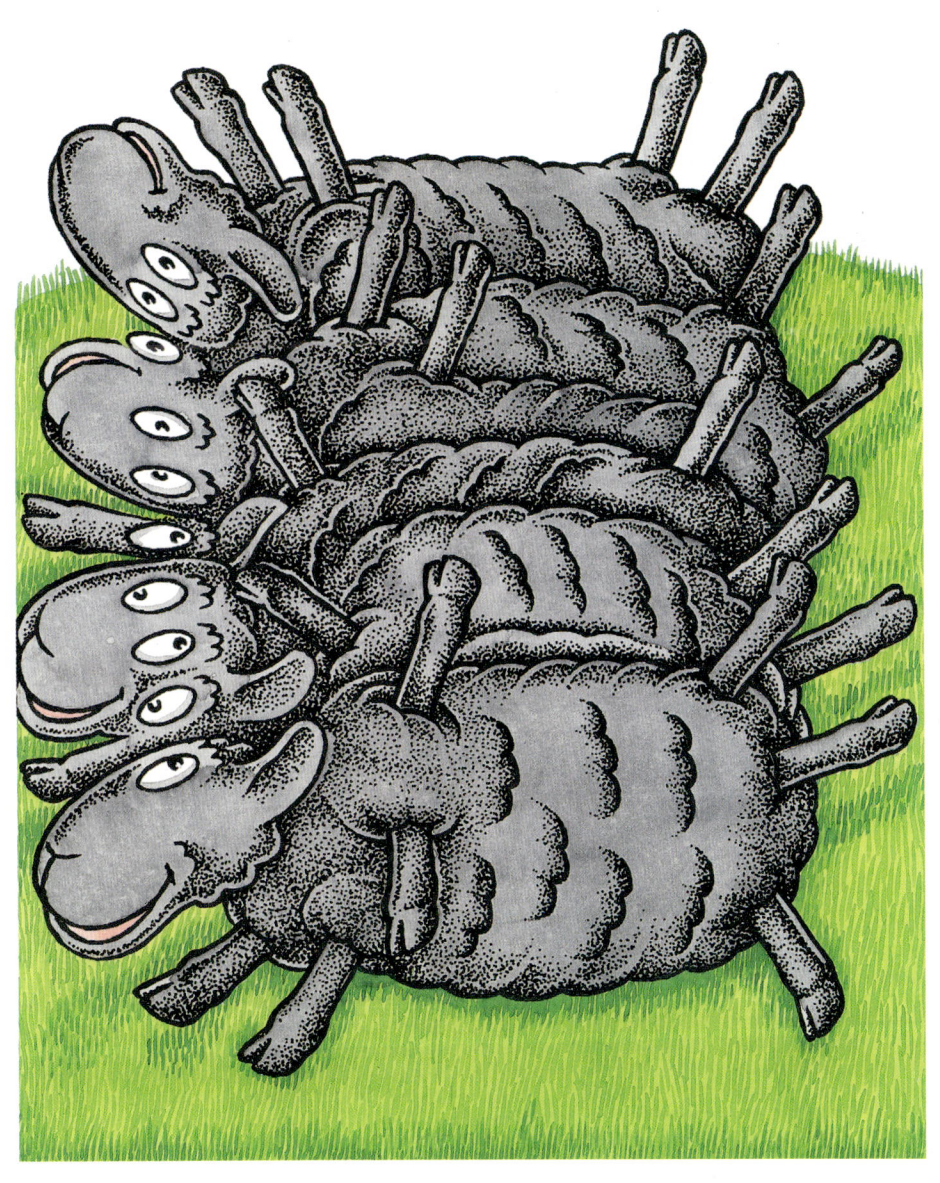

"Roll, Max, roll,"
said Min and Mop.

The fox ran away.

Max still rolls.
But he eats grass too.